English Song
Renaissance to Baroque

Low Voice

Edited by Steven Stolen and Richard Walters

On the cover: William Hogarth, British, 1697-1764, *The Enraged Musician,* engraving on ivory laid paper, 1741, 42 x 55.5 cm, Restricted gift of Mr. and Mrs. Joseph R. Shapiro, 1992.1
© 1996, The Art Institute of Chicago, All Rights Reserved.

ISBN 0-7935-4633-8

HAL•LEONARD® CORPORATION
7777 W. BLUEMOUND RD. P.O. BOX 13819 MILWAUKEE, WI 53213

Copyright © 1996 by HAL LEONARD CORPORATION
International Copyright Secured   All Rights Reserved

For all works contained herein:
Unauthorized copying, arranging, adapting, recording or public performance is an infringement of copyright.
Infringers are liable under the law.

Editors' Preface

We have suggested ornamentation that is stylistically appropriate, as well as being vocally comfortable for most singers. The songs are perfectly acceptable without ornamentation. The printed suggestions, always in smaller sized notes, will be a starting place for some singers. There are many further possibilities. Any ornaments and melodic embellishments should be pursued with complete regard to the individual singer's voice and comfortability. In embellishing the music of this period the melody can be decorated, but not obscured in the singer's ornamentation. The aim is to create spontaneity and a spirit of improvisation in a performance.

As a general guideline, in strophic songs ornamentation is added in later verses, particularly in refrains. In *da capo* arias ornamentation is added on the repeat of the first section of music.

Contents

Anonymous
- 8   Have You Seen But a White Lily Grow?
- 12 Pastime With Good Company
- 10 Willow Song

Thomas Arne
- 16 Blow, Blow, Thou Winter Wind
- 18 O Come, O Come, My Dearest
- 13 Thou Soft Flowing Avon
- 20 When Daisies Pied

John Bartlet
- 22 Whither Runneth My Sweetheart?

John Blow
- 25 Tell Me No More

Thomas Campian
- 28 Fair, If You Expect Admiring
- 30 Jack and Joan

John Dowland
32 Flow My Tears
31 Weep You No More, Sad Fountains
34 What If I Never Speed?

Thomas Ford
38 Since First I Saw Your Face

Orlando Gibbons
36 The Silver Swan

George Frideric Handel
42 Come and Trip It
39 Here Amid the Shady Woods
46 Let Me Wander Not Unseen
48 Where E'er You Walk

Tobias Hume
52 Fain Would I Change That Note

Robert Johnson
51 As I Walked Forth One Summer Day

Robert Jones
54 In Sherwood Lived Stout Robin Hood

Henry Lawes
56 How Happy Art Thou

Thomas Morley
58 It Was a Lover and His Lass

George Munro
57 My Lovely Celia

Francis Pilkington
62 Diaphenia
60 Rest Sweet Nymphs

Henry Purcell
66 Hark! The Echoing Air
70 I Attempt from Love's Sickness
74 I'll Sail Upon the Dog Star
76 If Music Be the Food of Love
63 Nymphs and Shepherds

Philip Rosseter
78 When Laura Smiles

As the son of an upholsterer, coffin maker, and erstwhile Handel opera producer, **Thomas Arne** (1710–1778) was part of a colorful and musical family. Arne gave his sister and younger brother voice lessons, and his wife was also a singer. His illegitimate son, Michael, was a composer and wrote the famous song "The Lass with the Delicate Air." Arne played lute and violin and was a self-taught composer. He had strong interest in the stage and had tremendous success as a composer of operas and masques. The song "Rule, Britannia" was from his masque *Alfred*, written in 1740. Other notable compositions include *Rosamond* (1733), *Dido and Aeneas* (1733), *Comus* (1738), some twenty-five books of songs, and numerous instrumental works, often featuring organ or harpsichord. In 1744 he was appointed resident composer at Drury Lane Theatre in London and held that post until a disagreement with a singer/actor prompted him to leave for Covent Garden in 1760. At Drury Lane, Arne received particular attention and acclaim for his settings of Shakespearean texts. He received an honorary doctorate from Oxford in 1759, hence the often-used title of Doctor Arne.

Little is known of **John Bartlet** (15??–16??), a man overshadowed both in fame and in ability by contemporaries such as Dowland and Gibbons. He seems to have been employed in the service of Sir Edward Seymour, Earl of Hartford, and received a B.Mus. degree from Oxford in 1610. A collection of lute songs that he published in 1606 contains his only known works.

John Blow (1649–1708) received his early education at the Magnus Song School in Newark. The early teacher of Henry Purcell, he was a chorister at the Chapel Royal in London. In 1668 he became organist at Westminster Abbey. He succeeded Pelham Humfrey as Master of the Children at Chapel Royal in 1674 and held that position until his death. Blow also returned to his position as organist at Westminster Abbey following Purcell's death in 1695. Blow's greatest contributions to the vocal repertory come from his service music, with over 100 English anthems, numerous welcome odes, five odes for St. Cecilia's Day, coronation anthems for James II and for William and Mary, and odes for the deaths of Queen Mary (1695) and Henry Purcell (1696). Blow also composed a masque, *Venus and Adonis* (1685), and a collection of songs, *Amphion Anglicus* (1700).

In addition to his contributions as a composer, **Thomas Campian** (1567–1620) was a well-known and widely traveled scholar, physician, and theorist. In 1605 he received his M.D. from the University of Caen and began practicing medicine in London. Much of his early creative years were as a poet, and his verses were set by many of his songwriting contemporaries. His first collection of ayres (with works by Philip Rosseter) was published in 1601, and four more collections were published between 1613 and 1617. In 1613 he published a book on counterpoint, and he had many of his poetic works, including the poetry in *Songs of Mourning*, on the death of Prince Henry, set by Coprario. Campian the composer set only his own texts, employing a simple approach to the vocal line, so as to preserve the poetic meter.

With the creation or invention of the "ayre" **John Dowland** (1563–1626) stands at the forefront of early composers of song. The ayre is a simple form where the primary interest is in the top voice. The other voices are usually written in choral style and could have been sung in that fashion, but were preferably performed by solo voice and lute. Dowland was both singer and lutenist and traveled widely, performing his music and learning about art and style throughout Europe. His early years were marked by a period of service in Paris, working for the English ambassador, Henry Dobham. In 1580, while in

Dobham's service, Dowland converted to Roman Catholicism. He returned to England in 1584, married, and tried to gain a position in Elizabeth's court. Unsuccessful, he began a period of travel that lasted until 1609, including time in Germany and Italy. Near the end of the century, Dowland returned both to Protestantism and to England, but again was unsuccessful professionally, so he went to Denmark as court musician to Christian IV in 1598. Dowland often complained of his lack of success in England because of his acceptance abroad. It was, however, his cosmopolitan background that made his music widely known and gave it such lasting impact. His works include three volumes of lute songs (1597–1603), a set of instrumental pavans entitled *Lachrymae*, and a collection of songs with viol and lute accompaniment, *A Pilgrimes Solace*.

Thomas Ford (1580–1648) entered into the service of Henry, Prince of Wales, in 1611 and was appointed one of the musicians to Charles I in 1626. "Since First I Saw Your Face" is from an anthology published by Ford in 1607 called *Musicke of Sundrie Kindes*. In addition to lute songs, the collection features catches, rounds, and other pieces intended to be performed by four voices. The work was sold in St. Dunstan's Courtyard, Fleet Street, the home church of many lute song composers of the time.

Orlando Gibbons (1583–1625) came from a musical family in Oxford. His grandfather Richard was a chamberlain of the city, and his father, William, was well known as a musician. At the age of twelve, Gibbons joined the choir at King's College, Cambridge, where his brother Edward was master of the choristers. In 1605 he was appointed organist at the Chapel Royal and held this position until his death. Oxford awarded him a doctorate in 1622, and he was appointed organist at Westminster Abbey the following year. He died suddenly at Canterbury while waiting to render his services at the marriage of Charles I. More notable as a keyboard player and composer for harpsichord and organ, and for his service music and anthems, Gibbons was a fine writer of madrigals in the traditional style. He left only thirteen in a published collection (1612), of which "The Silver Swan" is the most famous. Although originally written in five-part choral form, it has become a solo song in the tradition of the lute ayre.

George Frideric Handel (orig. Georg Friedrich Handel; 1685–1759) received his early training on the harpsichord and violin in Halle, the city of his birth. His first productions, of the operas *Almira* and *Nero*, were mounted in 1705 in Hamburg. Handel was a cosmopolitan man and traveled Europe—specifically, Italy, from 1706 to 1709. These years marked the successful premiere of the opera *Agrippina* (1709) in Venice, as well as the oratorio *La resurrezione* (1708) and Handel's emergence as a virtuoso organist and harpsichordist. In 1710 he assumed the position of Kapellmeister to the Elector of Hanover, but obtained leaves of absence for trips to London. When the Elector of Hanover became George I of England in 1714, Handel decided to stay in London for good. He founded his own company, the Royal Academy of Music, in 1720, and in 1726 became a British citizen, officially changing his name to George Frideric. The popularity of John Gay's *The Beggar's Opera* in 1728, combined with the competition from Italians like Bononcini, undermined Handel's early operatic success, and he went bankrupt. In the 1730s he turned to the oratorio and was tremendously successful. *Esther* (1732) was followed by *Deborah*, *Saul*, and *Israel in Egypt*. *Messiah* (1742) and the twelve oratorios he composed thereafter further ensured his security as a composer of oratorio. The oratorio more than made up for his financial losses as a composer and producer of operas, and Handel was a wealthy man at the time of his death. Individual arias from his operas and oratorios have had perennial appeal, and although they were originally composed for specific voices and characters, many have transposed easily to become a traditional part of the song repertory and suitable for any voice.

Although **Tobias Hume** (1569–1645) is known as a composer, he considered himself an amateur in this area and was in truth a full-time soldier. Despite his protestations, Hume was an excellent gambist and wrote two collections of viol music and songs (*Musicall Humours and Poeticall Musicke*, 1605 and 1607). His peculiar and eccentric personality has led historians to believe that he was the model for the character Sir Andrew Agrecheck in *Twelfth Night*.

Robert Johnson (1583–1633) was the son of lutenist and composer John Johnson. He was appointed lutenist to James I in 1604 and retained that position under Charles I. In addition to his lute songs, Johnson provided music and songs for stage works, including Shakespeare's *The Tempest* and Fletcher's *The Mad Lover*.

Robert Jones (1565–1616) was a noted composer of Jacobean ayres (later known as ballads). Between 1600 and 1610 he had five books of ayres and one book of madrigals published. Unhappy with his lack of success, he changed artistic directions and went into business with colleague Philip Rosseter to train young actors and promote Children of Whitefriars, a children's acting troupe.

Henry Lawes (1596–1662), like many other lute song composers, was a singer and served as Gentleman of the Chapel Royal. In 1634 Lawes composed the music for Thomas Carew's masque *Coelum Britannicum* and was commissioned by the Earl of Bridgwater to do the same for Milton's *Comus*. He always showed a fondness for great writing and was a friend of Herrick, Walter, and Suckling and was, in 1645, the subject of a sonnet by Milton. In 1636 he was selected to write music for the king's visit to Oxford and later that year had the first of over 350 songs for voice and continuo published. Other works include an opera, *The Siege of Rhodes*, service music, Christmas songs in Herrick's *Hesperides*, and an elegy on the death of his musician brother, William.

Best known as the organist at St. Peter's, Cornhill (the "actor's church" in the City of London), **George Munro** (1685–1731) has not been accorded high standing as a composer. Nevertheless, "My Lovely Celia," easily his finest and most enduring song, has for centuries been a staple of the vocal repertory. Primarily a keyboard player, Munro was also a composer of popular songs, mostly during his time as harpsichordist at Goodman Fields Theatre.

Like many of his colleagues, **Thomas Morley** (c. 1557–1602) began his musical life as chorister, singing at St. Paul's Cathedral. He was an early pupil of William Byrd and received his music degree from Oxford in 1588. At about the same time, he became the organist at St Giles's Church, Cripplegate, in London. In 1589 he was appointed organist at St. Paul's, and in 1592 he became a Gentleman of the Chapel Royal. Morley, who lived in the same parish as Shakespeare, in 1599 provided the music to "It Was a Lover and His Lass" for *As You Like It*. His treatise *A Plaine and Easie Introduction to Practicall Musicke* was published in 1597. Morley was a well-known madrigalist and helped compile *The Triumphs of Oriana* (1601), a collection of madrigals in praise of Queen Elizabeth. He also composed service music in English and Latin, fancies for viols, and pieces for virginal.

Francis Pilkington (1570–1638) received a B.Mus. degree from Lincoln College, Oxford, in 1595. Also a clergyman, he took holy orders in 1612 and was ordained to the priesthood in 1614. A resident and chorister in Chester, his significant publications include a book of ayres (1604) and his second book of madrigals (1624).

From the time of John Dowland to the notable figures of the twentieth century, **Henry Purcell** (1659–1695) stands alone as the greatest British composer, and his death marked the end of any important musical contribution from an English composer for nearly 200 years. Like many of his contemporaries, he came from a musical family, which included his brother Daniel, an important composer of the period as well. Purcell was a chorister at the Chapel Royal at the age of ten. In 1673 he left this position and began his study with John Blow, succeeding him in 1679 as organist at Westminster Abbey. In these first years at Westminster Abbey, Purcell began composing in earnest and wrote his first music for a play, Nathaniel Lee's *Theodosius*. He went on to write music and songs for over fifty dramatic works. *Dido and Aeneas* (1689) was written for a production at a girl's school and was his only through-composed opera. The work remains the only real representative of the period still being performed as a regular part of the repertory today. Other operatic and semi-operatic works include *King Arthur* (1691), *The Fairy Queen* (1692), and *The Indian Queen* (1695). Other notable appointments during his brief career include service in 1682 as a Gentleman of the Chapel Royal, where he sang bass and served as one of three organists. He also became, in 1683, the Royal Repairman, to oversee who would build the new organ at Temple Church. In 1685 James II named him Royal Harpsichordist. Despite these court appointments, Purcell depended greatly on the theater for work, and his enduring legacy is found in those compositions. He did compose a large amount of church and service music, including the music for the funeral of Queen Mary in 1694. This music was performed at his own funeral just one year later. His vocal music includes the ode for St. Cecilia's Day *Hail, Bright Cecilia* (1692) and the songs contained in *Orpheus Britannicus*, a two-volume collection published after his death. He also wrote *Nine Fantasias* (1680), *Twelve Sonatas of Three Parts* (1683), *Musick's Handmaid* (1689) for harpsichord, and another collection published posthumously, *Lessons for the Harpsichord or Spinet, Suites No. 1–8*.

Although not a prolific composer, **Philip Rosseter** (1568–1623) was a close friend of the more notable Thomas Campian and John Dowland. He was appointed by James I as court lutenist and served in this capacity until his death. A simple, unpretentious composer, Rosseter also was an impresario of sorts, working with fellow composer Robert Jones for a group of child actors known as the Children of Whitefriars.

Have You Seen But a White Lily Grow?

Ben Johnson

Anonymous
early 17th century

[Slow] [dolce] [p]

Have you seen but a white lil-y grow_____ be-fore rude hands had touched it; have you mark'd_ but_ the_ fall of the snow be-fore the earth hath smudged it? Have you felt the wool of bea-ver or swan's-down ev-er, or have smelt of the bud of the

Copyright © 1996 by HAL LEONARD CORPORATION
All Rights Reserved International Copyright Secured

briar or the nard in the fire, or have tast-ed the bag of the bee? Oh, so white, Oh, so soft, Oh, so sweet, so sweet. so sweet is she. Oh, so white, Oh, so soft, Oh so sweet so sweet, so sweet is she.

*optional melodic ornamentation by the editors

Willow Song

Anonymous
early 17th century

[Moderately slow]

The poor soul sat sighing by a sycamore tree.
He sigh'd in his singing and made a great moan.
The mute bird sat by him was made tame by his moans.
Take this for my farewell And latest adieu:

Sing willow, willow, willow.
Sing all a green willow.
Sing all a green willow.
Sing all a green willow.

With his hand on his bosom and his head upon her
I am dead to all pleasure My true love is
The true tears fell from him would have melted the
Write this on my tomb: that in love I was

11

Pastime With Good Company

Anonymous, 16th century
attributed to King Henry VIII

Thou Soft Flowing Avon

words by David Garrick

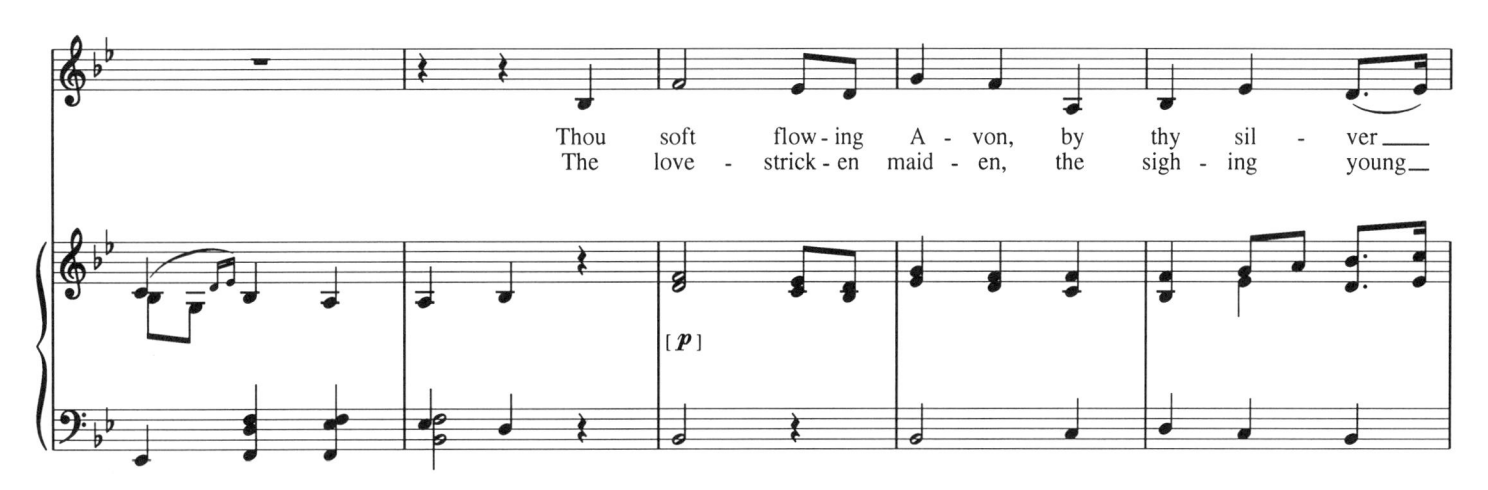

Thomas Arne

[Larghetto]

[mf]

[p]

Thou soft flow-ing A- von, by thy sil- ver
The love- strick- en maid- en, the sigh- ing young

*The editors' optional melodic ornamentation is for verse 2.

bed__ For hal-low'd the turf is which pil-low'd_ his_ head, The fair-ies by moon-light dance round his green_ bed,__ For hal-low'd the_ turf is_ which_ pil-low'd his_ head.

[mf]

Blow, Blow, Thou Winter Wind

words from *As You Like It*,
William Shakespeare

Thomas Arne
1740

1. Blow, blow, thou winter wind, Thou art not so unkind, thou art not so unkind As man's ingratitude. Thy

2. Freeze, freeze thou bitter sky, Thou dost not bite so nigh, thou dost not bite so nigh As benefits forgot, Tho'

*In each of the verses, the two large sections
(measures 9-16, measures 17-32) may each be repeated.*

Copyright © 1998 HAL LEONARD CORPORATION
All Rights Reserved   International Copyright Secured

tooth is not so keen — Because thou art not seen, thy
thou the waters warp — Thy sting is not so sharp, thy

tooth is not so keen — because thou art not seen, Al-
sting is not so sharp — As friend remembered not, thy

though thy breath be rude, although thy breath be rude, — al-
sting is not so sharp as friend remembered not, — as

1. though thy breath be rude.
2. friend remembered not.

[mf]

O Come, O Come, My Dearest

from the pantomime *The Fall of Phaeton*

words by Pritchard

Thomas Arne
1736

*Dynamics throughout reflect tutti (b.f.) and continuo (b.f.).

(tr)
fra - grant_a - toms_blend, Which in_a_gale of joy,_ which in a_gale of joy_ thy
[p] [mf]
breath_ at - tend._ Thy love in gen - tle mur-murs to my soul_ ap - ply, Heal me with kiss-es, oh!
heal_ me_with_kiss-es, or_ else_ I_ die,_ or_ else_ I die.
[mf]

When Daisies Pied

words from *Love's Labour Lost,* William Shakespeare

Thomas Arne

[Moderately]

1. When daisies pied, and violets blue, And ladysmocks all silver white, And cuckoo buds of yellow hue, Do paint the meadows with delight:
2. When shepherds pipe on oaten straws, And merry larks are ploughmen's clocks, And turtles tread, and rooks, and daws, And maidens bleach their summer frocks:

The cuck-oo then, on ev-'ry tree, Mocks mar-ried men, mocks mar-ried men, mocks mar-ried men; for thus sings he: Cuck-oo, cuck-oo, cuck-oo, cuck-oo, cuck-oo! O word of fear, O word of fear, Un-pleas-ing to a mar-ried ear, un-pleas-ing to a mar-ried ear.

* optinal melodic ornamentation for verse 2, by the editors
** appogiatura possible

Whither Runneth My Sweetheart?

John Bartlet
1606

[Moderately Fast]

Whith-er run-neth my sweet-heart? Whith-er run-neth my sweet-heart? Stay, stay, stay, stay and take me with thee. Mer-ri-ly, mer-ri-ly, mer-ri-ly I'll play my part. Stay, stay, and thou shalt see me, and thou shalt see me, and thou shalt see me, and thou shalt see me. Oh! oh!

Have I ketcht, have I ketcht thee? Have I ketcht, have I ketcht thee? Hay ding-a-ding-a-ding, Hay ding-a-ding-a-ding, Hay ding-a-ding-a-ding, Hay ding-a-ding-a-ding, This ketch-ing is ___ a pret-ty thing, This ketch-

-ing is a pret-ty thing. Oh! oh! Have I ketcht, have I ketcht thee? Have I ketcht, have I ketcht thee? Hay ding-a-ding-a-ding, Hay ding-a-ding-a-ding, Hay ding-a-ding-a-ding, Hay ding-a-ding-a-ding, This ketch-ing is a pret-ty thing, This ketch-ing is a pret-ty thing.

Tell Me No More

John Blow

[Moderately]

Tell me no more, no more you love; in vain, fair Celia, tell me no more, no more you love; in vain, fair Celia, in vain, fair Celia, you this passion feign. Tell me no more, no

more you love. Can they pretend to love, who do refuse what love persuades them to? Tell me no more, no more you love. Who once has felt his active fire, dull laws of honour will disdain. Tell me no more, no more you love; in vain, fair Celia you would be thought, you would be thought, you would be thought his slave; and yet you will not, and yet you will not to his pow'r submit.

Tell me no more, no more you love; in vain, fair Ce - lia, in vain, fair Ce - lia you this pas - sion feign.

Fair, If You Expect Admiring

Thomas Campian
1601

Fair, if you expect admiring,
Sweet, if you provoke desiring,
Grace dear love with kind requiting.
Fond, but if thy sight be blindness,
False, if thou affect unkindness,
Fly both love and love's delighting.

Fates, if you rule lovers' fortunes,
Stars, if men your pow'rs importune,
Yield relief by your relenting.
Time, if Sorrow be not endless,
Hope made vain, and Pity friendless,
Help to ease my long lamenting.

* appoggiatura possible
** The editors' optional ornamentation is for verse 2.

love's de - light - ing. Then when hope is lost and
long la - ment - ing. But if griefs re - main still

love is scorn - ed I'll bu - ry my de - sires and quench the fires That
un - re - dress - ed I'll fly to her a - gain and sue for pi - ty

ev - er yet in vain have burn - ed. I'll bu - ry my de - sires and
to re - new my hopes dis - tress - ed. I'll fly to her a - gain and

quench the fires That ev - er yet in vain have burn - ed.
sue for pi - ty to re - new my hopes dis - tress - ed.

Jack and Joan

Thomas Campian

[Fast]

Jack and Joan they think no ill, But loving live, and merry still; Do their week days' work, and pray Devoutly on the holy day: Skip and trip it on the green, And help to choose the Summer Queen; Lash out at a country feast, Their silver penny with the best.

Well can they judge of nappy ale, And tell at large a winter tale, Climb up to the apple loft, And turn the crabs till they be soft. Tib is all the father's joy, And little Tom the mother's boy, All their pleasure is content, And care to pay their yearly rent.

Joan can call by name her cows, And deck her windows with green boughs. She can wreaths and tutties make, And trim with plums a bridal cake. Jack knows what brings gain or loss, And his long flail can stoutly toss; Make the hedge which others break, And ever thinks what he doth speak.

Now you courtly dames and knights, That study only strange delights, Though you scorn the home-spun grey, And revel in your rich array. Though your tongues dissemble deep, And can your heads from danger keep; Yet for all your pomp and train, Securer lives the silly swain.

Weep You No More, Sad Fountains

John Dowland
1603

[Rather slow; expressively]

[mp]

1. Weep ___ you no more, sad foun-tains; What need you flow so fast?
2. Sleep ___ is a re-con-cil-ing, A rest that Peace be-gets.

Look ___ how the snow-y moun-tains Heaven's sun doth gent-ly waste. But my sun's ___
Doth ___ not the sun rise smil-ing When fair at e'en he sets? Rest you then, ___

___ heav'n-ly eyes View not your weep-ing, That now lies sleep-ing,
___ rest, sad eyes, Melt not in weep-ing While she lies sleep-ing,

that now lies sleep-ing, Soft-ly, soft-ly, now soft-ly lies ___ sleep-ing.
while she lies sleep-ing, Soft-ly, soft-ly, now soft-ly lies ___ sleep-ing.

* *The repeat is within each of the two verses.*

Copyright © 1996 by HAL LEONARD CORPORATION
All Rights Reserved International Copyright Secured

Flow My Tears

John Dowland
1600

[Slow]

Flow my tears fall from your springs, Ex-il'd
for ev-er let me mourn: Where night's black bird her
sad in-fa-my sings, There let me live for-lorn.

Down vain lights shine you no more, No nights
are dark e-nough for those That in de-spair their
last for-tunes de-plore, Light doth but shame dis-close.

Nev-er may my woes be re-liev-ed, Since pit-y is fled,
From the high-est spire of con-tent-ment, My for-tune is thrown,

And tears, and sighs, and groans my weary days, my weary days
And fear, and grief, and pain for my deserts, for my deserts

Of all joys have deprived.
Are my hopes since hope is gone.

Hark you shadows that in darkness dwell, Learn to contemn light,

Happy, happy they that in hell Feel not the world's despite.

What If I Never Speed?

John Dowland
1603

[Moderately]

1. What if I never speed? Shall I straight yield to de-spair, And still on sor-row feed, That can no loss re-pair?
   Or shall I change my love? For I can find pow'r to de-part, And in my rea-son prove I can com-mand my heart.
2. Oft I have dream'd of joy, Yet I never felt the sweet, But tired with an-noy, My griefs each oth-er meet.
   Oft I have left my hope, As a wretch by fate for-lorn, But Love aims at one scope, And lost will still re-turn.

But if she will pi-ty my de-sire, and

Copyright © 1996 by HAL LEONARD CORPORATION
International Copyright Secured   All Rights Reserved

_____ my love re - quite, then ev - er shall she live my dear de - light. Come, come, come, while I have a heart to de - sire thee, Come, come, come, for eith - er I will love or ad - mire thee.

The Silver Swan

Orlando Gibbons
published 1612

last, and sang no more. Fare-well all joys, O death, come close mine eyes. More geese than swans now live, more fools than wise! Fare-well all joys, O death, come close mine eyes. More geese than swans now live, more fools than wise!

[rit.]

Since First I Saw Your Face

Thomas Ford
1607

[Moderately]

Since first I saw your face I re-solv'd To hon-our and re-nown ye. If now I be dis-
I ad - mire or praise you too much, That fault you may for - give me. Or if my hands had
sun whose beams most glo - ri - ous are Re - ject - eth no be - hold - er; And your sweet beau - ty

dain - ed I wish My heart had nev - er known ye. What, I that lov'd and you that lik'd Shall we be - gin to
stray'd but a touch, Then just - ly might you leave me. I ask'd you leave, you bade me love, Is't now a time to
past com - pare Made my poor eyes the bold - er. Where Beau - ty moves and Wit de - lights And signs of kind - ness

wran - gle? No, no, no, my heart is fast, And can - not dis - en - tan -
chide me? No, no, no, I'll love you still What for - tune e'er be - tide
bind me, There, o there, where e'er I go, I'll leave my heart be - hind

[1,2] [3]

gle. No, no, no, my heart is fast, And can - not dis - en - tan - gle. 2. If me.
me. No, no, no, I'll love you still what for - tune e'er be - tide me. 3. The
me. There, o there, where'er I go, I'll leave my heart be - hind

* *The editors' optional melodic ornamentation is for verse 2 or 3.*

Copyright © 1996 by HAL LEONARD CORPORATION
All Rights Reserved   International Copyright Secured

Here Amid the Shady Woods

from the oratorio *Alexander Balus*

words by Thomas Morell

George Frideric Handel
1748

soul, this charm-ing seat,___ Love and glo - ry's calm__ re - treat.

Here a - mid the sha - dy woods,____ Taste, my

soul, this charm - ing seat, Love and glo - ry's calm re - treat.____

Here a - mid the sha - dy woods, Fra - grant flow'rs__ and crys - tal floods, Taste, my soul, this calm re-treat Love and glo-ry's calm re-treat, taste, my soul, this charm-ing seat, love and glo-ry's calm re-treat, love and glo-ry's calm re-treat.

[f]

* *appoggiatura possible*
** *optional melodic variations by the editors*

Come and Trip It

from the oratorio *L'Allegro*

words by Jennens, compiled from Milton

George Frideric Handel
1740

optional melodic ornamentation by the editors

tas-tic toe, on the ___ light fan-tas-tic ___ toe! Come, and trip ___ it

as __ you go, come, and trip __ it as __ you go,

on the light fan-tas-tic toe, trip it, trip it, trip it, trip it

as __ you go, _____ on __ the light _ fan-tas-tic toe;

come, and trip it as you go, trip it, trip it, on the light fantastic toe, come, come, come, come, and trip it as you go, on the light fantastic toe, on the light fantastic toe!

Let Me Wander Not Unseen

from the oratorio *L'Allegro, il Penseroso ed il Moderato*

words by Jennens,
compiled from Milton

George Frideric Handel
1740

land. And the milk-maid sing-eth blithe, And the mow-er whets his scythe, And ev-er-y shep-herd tells his tale, Un-der the haw-thorn in the dale, And ev-er-y shep-herd tells his tale, Un-der the haw-thorn in the dale.

Where E'er You Walk

from the oratorio *Semele*

words by William Congreve

George Frideric Handel
1744

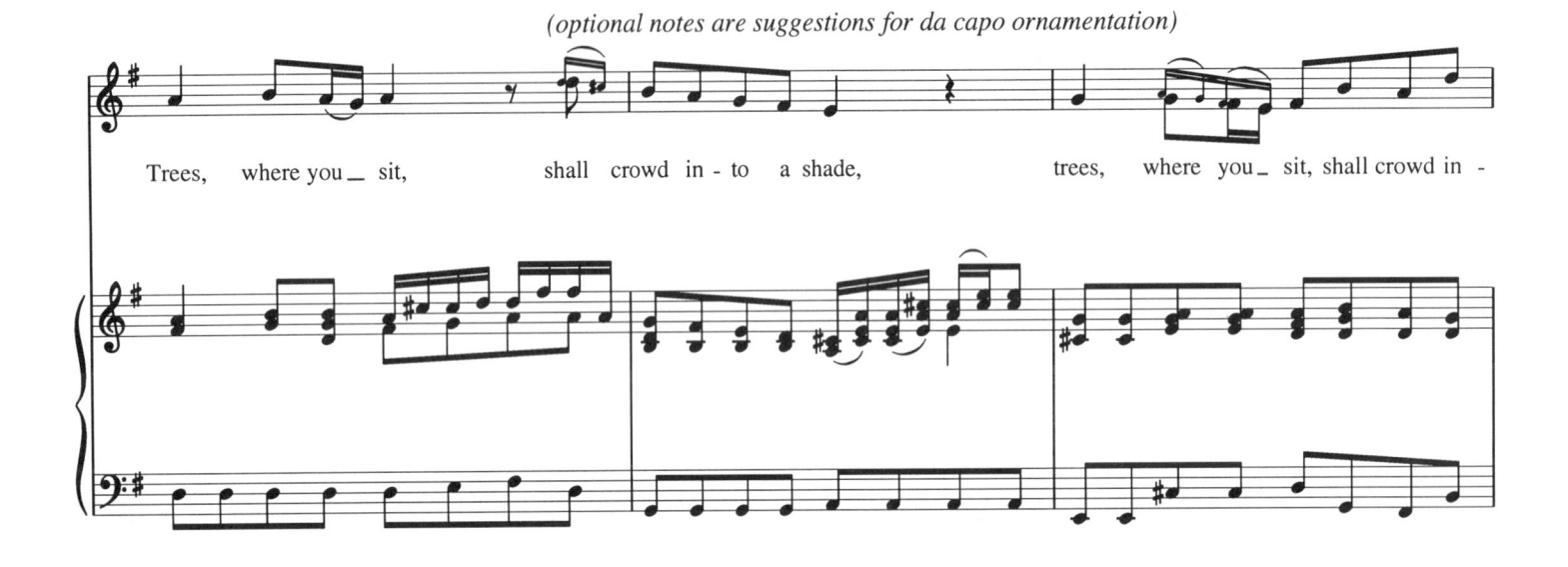

*appoggiatura possible on da capo

gales shall fan the glade; Trees, where you sit, shall crowd in-to a shade,

trees, where you sit, shall crowd in-

to a shade. **Fine**

Where e'er you tread, the blushing flow'rs shall rise, And all things flour-ish, and all things flour-ish where e'er you turn your eyes, where e'er you turn your eyes, where e'er you turn your eyes.

[Adagio] Da Capo

(opt.: play R.H. 8va)

As I Walked Forth One Summer Day

Robert Johnson
1659

[Moderately]

1. As I walk'd forth one summer's day, To view the meadows green and gay, A pleasant bow-er I espied, Standing fast by the river side, And in't a maiden I heard cry, Alas, alas, there's none e'er lov'd as I.

2. Then round the meadow did she walk, Catching each flower by the stalk, Such flow'rs as in the meadow grew, The dead-man's thumb, and herb all blue, And as she pull'd them still cried she, Alas, alas, there's none e'er lov'd like me.

3. The flow'rs of the sweetest scents She bound about with knotty bents, And as she bound them up in bands, She wept, she sigh'd, and wrung her hands: Alas! Alas! Alas! cried she, Alas, alas, there's none e'er lov'd like me.

4. When she had filled her apron full Of such green things as she could cull; The green leaves served her for her bed, The flow'rs were a pillow for her head; Then down she laid, ne'er more did speak, Alas, alas, with love her heart did break.

Fain Would I Change That Note

Tobias Hume
1605

*The editors' optional melodic ornamentation is for verse 2.

Copyright © 1996 by HAL LEONARD CORPORATION
All Rights Reserved   International Copyright Secured

come, _____ Love is the per - fect sum _____
bliss, _____ Where tru - est plea - sure is, _____

___ Of all de - light, _____ I have no
___ I do a - dore thee. _____ I know thee

oth - er choice _____ Ei - ther for pen or
what thou art, _____ I serve thee with my

voice _____ To sing or write. _____
heart _____ And fall be - fore thee. _____

appoggiatura possible

In Sherwood Lived Stout Robin Hood

Robert Jones
1609

In Sher-wood lived stout Ro-bin Hood, An arch-er great, none great-er, His bow and shafts were sure and good, Yet Cu-pid's were much bet-ter. Ro-bin could shoot at ma-ny a heart and miss; Cu-pid at

A no-ble thief was Ro-bin Hood, Wise was he could de-ceive him; Yet Mar-ian in his brav-est mood Could of his heart be-reave him. No great-er thief lies hid-den un-der skies Than Beau-ty

An out-law was this Ro-bin Hood, His life free and un-ru-ly; Yet to fair Mar-ian bound he stood, And love's debt paid her du-ly. Whom curb of strict-est law could not hold in, Love with o-

Now wend we home, stout Ro-bin Hood, Leave we the woods be-hind us. Love pas-sions must not be with-stood, Love ev-'ry-where will find us. I lived in field and town and so did he; I got me

55

first could hit a heart of his.
close - ly lodged in wo - men's eyes.
beyed - ness and a wink could win.
to the woods; Love fol - lowed me.

Hey! jol - ly Ro - bin, Ho! jol - ly Ro - bin, Hey! jol - ly Ro - bin Hood! Love finds out me As well as Thee To fol - low me, to fol - low me, to fol - low me, to fol - low me to the green wood.

* *The editors' optional melodic ornamentation is for verse 3 or 4.*

How Happy Art Thou

Henry Lawes

[Moderately fast]

How hap-py art thou and I, That nev-er knew how to love! There's no such bless-ing here be-neath What-e'er there is a-bove. 'Tis lib-er-ty, 'tis lib-er-ty That ev-'ry wise man knows.

Out, out up-on those eyes That think to mur-der me, And he's an ass be-lieves her fair That is not kind and free. There's noth-ing sweet, there's noth-ing sweet To man but lib-er-ty.

I'll tie my heart to none, Nor yet con-fine mine eyes, But I will play my game so well I'll nev-er want a prize. 'Tis lib-er-ty, 'tis lib-er-ty Has made me now thus wise.

My Lovely Celia

George Munro

The editors' optional melodic ornamentation is for verse 2 or 3.

It Was a Lover and His Lass

words from *As You Like It*,
William Shakespeare

Thomas Morley

[Lively]

1. It was a lov-er and his lass,
2. Be-tween the a-cres of the rye,
3. This car-ol they be-gan that hour,
4. Then, pret-ty lov-ers, take the time,

With a hey, and a ho, and a hey non-ie no, and a hey _____ non-ie non-ie no,

That o'er the green corn-field did pass
These pret-ty coun-try fools did lie
How that life was but a flow'r
For love is crown-ed with the prime

In spring-time, in spring-time, in spring-time, The on-ly pret-ty ring-time, When

* *The editors' optional melodic ornamentation is for verse 3 or 4.*

Copyright © 1996 by HAL LEONARD CORPORATION
All Rights Reserved   International Copyright Secured

birds do sing, hey ding-a-ding-a-ding, hey ding-a-ding-a-ding, hey ding-a-ding-a-ding, Sweet lovers love the spring! In spring-time, in spring-time, The only pretty ring-time, When birds do sing, hey ding-a-ding-a-ding, hey ding-a-ding-a-ding, hey ding-a-ding-a-ding, Sweet lovers love the spring.

2. Be- spring.
3. This
4. Then,

Rest Sweet Nymphs

Francis Pilkington

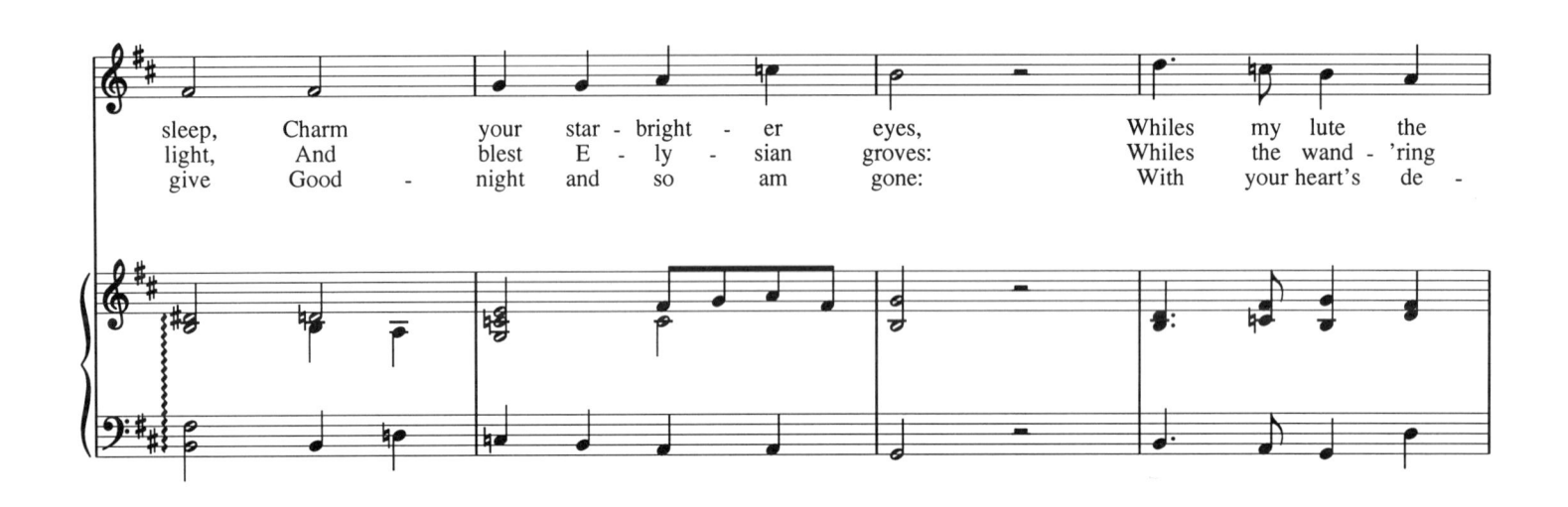

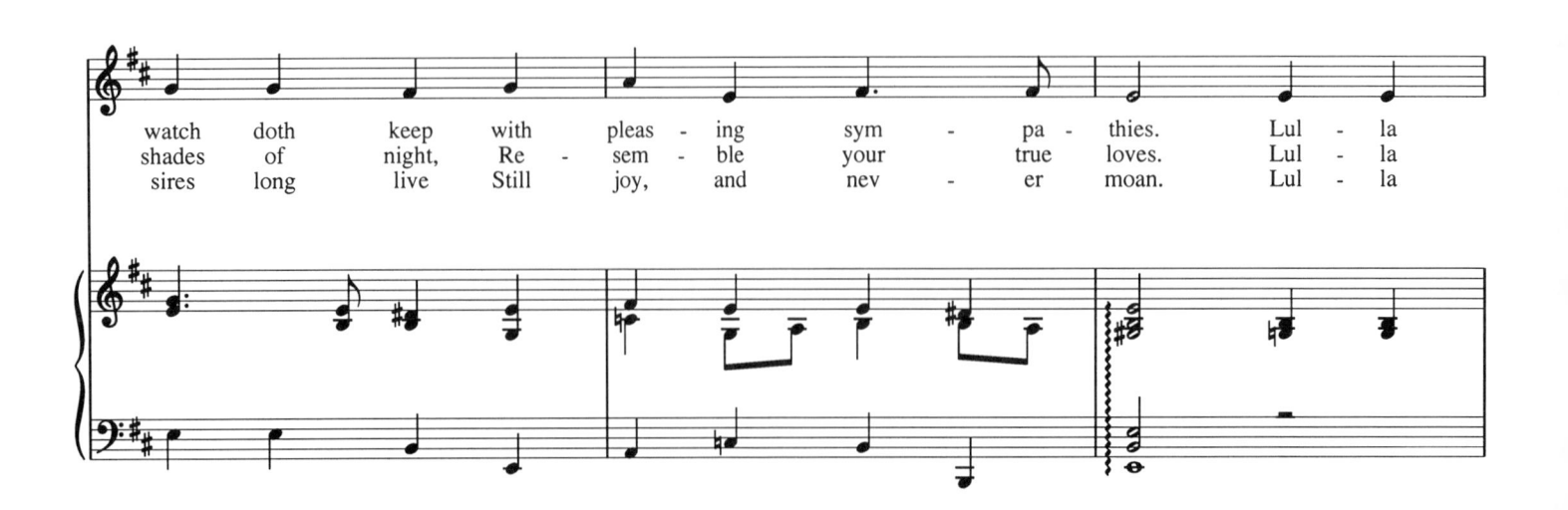

[Moderately]

Rest sweet Nymphs let gold-en sleep, Charm your star-bright-er eyes, Whiles my lute the watch doth keep with pleas-ing sym-pa-thies. Lul-la

Dream fair vir-gins of de-light, And blest E-ly-sian groves: Whiles the wand-'ring shades of night, Re-sem-ble your true loves. Lul-la

Thus dear dam-sels I do give Good-night and so am gone: With your heart's de-sires long live Still joy, and nev-er moan. Lul-la

61

Sleep sweet-ly, Sleep sweet-ly, Let no-thing af-fright ye, In calm con-tent-ments lie. Lul-la lul-la-by,
Your kiss-es, Your bliss-es Send them by your wish-es, Al-though now they be not nigh. Lul-la lul-la-by.
Hath pleas'd you And eas'd you, And sweet slum-ber seiz'd you, And now to bed I hie.

Diaphenia

Francis Pilkington
1605

*This repeat within each verse, found in the original sources, is optional.

Nymphs and Shepherds
from the play *The Libertine*

words by T. Shadwell

Henry Purcell
c1692

Flora's ho-li-day, this is Flora's ho-li-day, Sa-cred to ease _____ and hap-py love, To danc-ing, to mu - sic, to danc-ing, to mu - - sic and to po-e-try; Your flocks may now, now, now, now, now, now,

65

now, now, now, now se - cure - ly rove ____ Whilst you ex - press, whilst you ex - press ____ your jol - li - ty.

Nymphs and Shep - herds, come a - way, come a - way,

Nymphs and Shep - herds, come a - way, come a - way, come, come, come, come a - way.

optional melodic ornamentation by the editors

Hark! The Echoing Air
from *The Fairy Queen*

words by E. Settle,
after *A Midsummer Night's Dream*,
William Shakespeare

Henry Purcell
1692

[Slow]

Hark! hark! the ech-oing air a tri - - umph sings, hark! the ech-oing air a tri - - - umph sings, a tri - - - umph, a tri - - - umph, tri - umph sings,

* optional melodic ornamentation by the editors
** appoggiatura possible

tri - - - umph, tri - umph sings_____

_____ a tri - - - umph, tri - umph_ sings

And all_____ a - round, and all_____ a - round pleas'd_____

Cu - pids clap_ their wings, clap, clap, clap, clap_ their wings; pleas'd_____ Cu - pids clap their
[alt: pleas - - - ed_]

wings; and all a-round, and all a-round, pleas'd
[alt: pleas - - - ed]

Cu-pids clap clap, clap, clap, clap their wings, clap, clap, clap, clap, clap, clap, clap their

wings, pleas'd Cu-pids clap their wings And all a-
[alt: pleas - - - ed]

wings.

I Attempt from Love's Sickness
from *The Indian Queen*

Henry Purcell
1695

[Minuet tempo]

I attempt from Love's sickness to fly in vain, Since I am myself my own fever, since I am myself my own fever and pain. No

*optional melodic ornamentation by the editors
**appoggiatura possible

self my own fe - ver, since I am my - self my own fe - ver and

pain. For Love has more power and less mer - cy than fate. To

make us seek ru - in. to make us seek ru - in and on those that

hate. I at - tempt from Love's sick - ness to fly in

vain. Since I am myself my own fever, since I am myself my own fever and pain. I attempt from Love's sickness to fly in vain, Since I am myself my own fever, since I am myself my own fever and pain.

I'll Sail Upon the Dog Star

from the play *The Fool's Preferment, or The Three Dukes of Dunstable*

words by D'Urfey

Henry Purcell
1688

* *Play slightly detached throughout.*

Copyright © 1996 by HAL LEONARD CORPORATION
All Rights Reserved   International Copyright Secured

tear___ the rain-bow from the sky, I'll tear___ the rain-bow from the sky, And tie,_____ and tie both ends to-ge-ther. The stars pluck from their orbs, too, the stars pluck from their orbs, too, And crowd them in my bud-get! And whe-ther I'm a roar - - - ing boy, a roar - ing boy, Let all,_____ let all the na - tions judge it.

If Music Be the Food of Love
(First Version)

Henry Purcell
1692

*appoggiatura possible
** optional melodic ornamentation by the editors

When Laura Smiles

words attributed to Thomas Campian

Philip Rosseter
1601

[Moderately]

When Lau - ra smiles her sight revives both night and day;
The wan - ton spi - rits that remain in fleet - ing air
Di - an - a's eyes are not ad - orn'd with great - er power
Love hath no fire but what he steals from her bright eyes.

The earth and heav - en views with de - light
Af - fect for pas - time to un - twine
Than Lau - ra's when she lifts a while
Time hath no power but that which in

The editors' optional melodic ornamentation is for verse 3 or 4.

Copyright © 1996 by HAL LEONARD CORPORATION
All Rights Reserved International Copyright Secured

her wanton play; And her speech with
her tress-ed hair; And the birds think
her plea-sure lies. For when she with her

ev-er-flow-ing mu-sic doth re-
sweet Au-ro-ra, Morn-ing's queen, doth
eyes en-clos-eth, blind-ness doth ap-
di-vine beau-ty all the world sub-

pair The cru-el wounds of sor-row
shine From her bright sphere, when Lau-ra
pear The chief-est grace of beau-ty
dues And fills with heaven-ly spi-rits

and un-tam'd des-pair.
shows her looks di-vine.
sweet-ly seat-ed there.
my hum-ble Muse.